Ilkeston

The
Past and Present
in
Pictures

1878 - 2018

Written & produced by Andrew Sanders

British Library Cataloguing in Publication Data.
A catalogue record for this book is available from the British Library.

ISBN 978 0 86071 759 1

Photos on front and rear cover:
The Sanders family property on the junction of Derby Road & South Street c.1905. It is believed that the gentleman stood in the doorway of his fruit and veg shop is my late Great Grandfather William Sanders. The Saunders / Sanders family had resided at this address from the late 1700's until its untimely demolition in 1933.

A Commissioned Publication Printed by

MOORLEYS
Print, Design & Publishing
info@moorleys.co.uk · www.moorleys.co.uk

Preface

This book is dedicated to those 'Ilkestonians' who hold fond memories of how the town once appeared, those who wish to reminisce of times gone by, the places they used to visit and had many a happy time.

It's also for those who have moved away who can remember the days of old, but have no idea of what the town appears like today.

Sit back, relax, and enjoy the journey from Heanor Road to Little Hallam Hill, visiting Manor Road, Manners Road, Victoria Park, Granby Street, Awsworth Road, Pelham Street, Lord Haddon Road, Bath Street, East Street, Burr Lane, Chapel Street, North Street, Station Road, Station Street, Upper & Lower Market Places, Pimlico, Market Street, South Street, White Lion Square, Stanton Road & finally onto Little Hallam Hill.

Acknowledgements

I'd like to say a big thank you to the following for their co-operation and use of their photographs in the production of this book.

Erewash Borough Council
Ilkeston Library
Matlock Library
York Library

Carl Aldred
John Bibbs
Kathleen Brown
Stephen Brown
Jean Richards / Kelly Centro
Nigel Clifton
John Cook
Russ Draper
Diana Else
Ivan Eyre
Bunney Hayes
Alan Hobson
Andrew Knighton
Peter Sanders

The Staff at Heron Foods

The late Fynger Cooper (Kevin Crowley) who had extensive knowledge of Ilkeston history

The Ilkeston & District Local History Society
Ilkeston – Past & Present in Pictures The Facebook Site
Ilson Bygones Facebook Site

Sincere apologies to anyone that I may have missed in the above list

Also thanks to my partner, Kay Lawson, who has supported me during the last two years, whilst I compiled this book

Heanor Road

Ilkeston General Hospital – Heanor Road
Built in 1893, this redbrick building was opened by Lord Belper.
It had separate wards for children, men & women. It had a single operating room, a mortuary and several outbuildings. This is now the Rutland Manor Nursing Home.
Photo c.1902.

The original site for Granby School chosen in Oct 1878 was in Potter's Old Engine Close which belonged to the Duke of Rutland. It was described as being a field on the south side of Charlotte Street about half way down the hill, but by February of the following year the Duke had made it quite clear that he didn't want to part with this land.

Two alternative sites were offered, one of those accepted by the Board was at the junction of Charlotte Street and Heanor Road.

The Granby schools finally opened for business during the second week of January 1883 though formally opened in April of that year by which time there were 470 children 'on the books'. They were built to accommodate 578 boys and girls but no infants.

Photo c.1902.

Pearl Insurance Company & Hickinbotham on the north side of Heanor Road and Granby Street junction. To this day the building is used by 'Hamilton's Schoolwear & Embroidery'.

Manor Road, Manners Road & Victoria Park

The Hudson Bros. Garage on lower Manor Road in 1957. Frank Hudson offering his services to one happy 1940's Morris car owner.

This garage is now run by long-term owner Jack Hand since 1969, he is one of Ilkeston's well reputed car mechanics. The garage is situated opposite the entrance to Aldi, the site of the Old Rutland Hotel.

Mines Rescue Station on Manners Road – photo taken c.1920. The station finally ceased operation in 1993 and was then converted into an old people's home.
Built on the site of an old pit, the underneath of the building became a training area for its employees with several tunnels stretching over hundreds of yards.

Victoria Park c.1909. The wrought-iron gates were closed at dusk, but this did not deter the local children from forcibly bending the railings to gain entry. The railings that surrounded the park were removed during the Second World War mainly for salvage.

Granby Street & Awsworth Road

Billboard to the north-east side of the old Copi-mate building (now Domino's Pizza) on the junction of Granby Street and Bath Street. The Rutland Hotel can be seen just behind the Felix Bus on Bath Street. Unsure as to whether this type of advertising would be deemed as being acceptable in this day and age.

This building on the corner of Awsworth Road and Cotmanhay Road was constructed in 1790, and is said to be one of Ilkeston's oldest buildings. It has had several uses over the years, but originally had connections with the church on the opposite side of the road. Rumour has it that they were once connected via a subterranean passage!

Pelham Street

Pelham Street as viewed from the junction with Lord Haddon Road. This street, as can be seen, has remained pretty much unchanged, except for the different businesses that have been & gone over the last 97+ years. Photo taken in 1920.

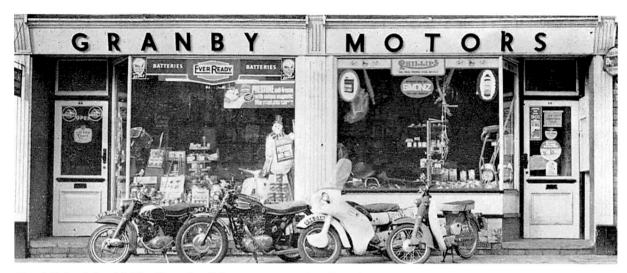

Established in 1965, **Granby Motors** was a leading independent motorcycle dealer serving Derbyshire & Nottinghamshire

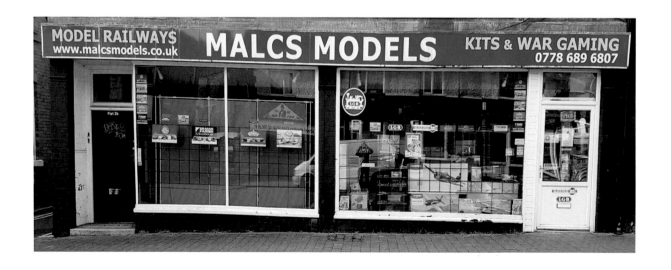

Lord Haddon Road

1903 - Workers re-surfacing the road.
Photo taken looking south from the junction of Lord Haddon and Manners Road, The Theatre Royal can be clearly seen on the right-hand side of the road.

Lord Haddon Road (circa.1906) looking north towards the junction with Manners Road. The Theatre Royal can be seen on the left hand side of the photo. The Theatre opened on Monday, 23rd December 1895, its first owner being a Mr. H Vincent Clarke. Some 20 years after opening, the building began to be used for the showing of motion pictures and became known as Vint's Electric Picturedrome.

Throughout the years 1916-26 it became known as the Coliseum.

Lord Haddon Road as viewed from the junction with Pelham Street – In 1926 the old theatre was demolished and a new theatre was built in its place, consequently this was known as New Theatre and operated as a theatre and cinema until 1963. With the increased number of televisions that appeared during the 1960's the theatre became unprofitable and it was eventually used as a carpet warehouse and also a place of worship until demolition started in 1984 (as shown).

The new site then became home to Haddon House Care Home at 38 Lord Haddon Road.

Bath Street

The old Mundy Arms stood two doors up from the junction of Bath Street and Granby Street. The business operated from circa. 1850 until the early 1990's when it was then converted into George's Tradition (fish & chip shop) as we know it today. These changes happened at roughly the same time as the Rutland Hotel was demolished. Photo taken in 1909.

Copi-mate and Servaset on the junction of lower Bath Street & Granby Street with the Mundy Arms to the right. In more recent years after the construction of Chalons Way (Ilkeston's Relief Road) the Mundy Arms closed and became George's Tradition fish and chip shop, Domino's Pizzas can be seen just to the left of it.

The Mundy Arms on lower Bath Street, now the site of George's Tradition chip shop. All of the buildings to the right having all disappeared around 1992/93 with the construction of Chalons Way and a large traffic island just to the east of where the Rutland Hotel once stood (now the site of Aldi Supermarket).

Lower Bath Street at the junction with Granby Street circa. 1905, note the lack of building where Hamilton's now stands, the buildings to the right and the different roof line on the Norton Plastics building.

The Rutland Hotel once stood on the bottom west side of Bath Street and first appeared in Pigot's Directory by 1830-31 with landlord listed as John Ives which was potentially a typo, and should have read 'Hives'. Hives was listed as running the Jolly Colliers from 1827-1829 but it is believed that the Colliers may have been renamed as the Rutland Hotel between 1829 and 1830 whilst the Baths were being built.

Wheldon's of Derby – Gift Shop in the early 1900's.

Later in the 1920's, these premises were taken over by Mrs Anna Maria Dampier and her daughter Annie, and operated as 'Dampier's' drapery shop until the late 1960's at which time was a babywear specialist.

During the mid-1990's it was operated by Coldseal Double Glazing, and in more recent years as a Newsagents under the name of 'Ilkeston News'.

Bath Street, Ilkeston

Newman Household Stores stood near the bottom of Bath Street to the right of the old train station.

Over the years this building has had several uses such as Everley's hardware store run by Pete Everley in the 60's and 70's, a car accessory and spares shop, Visage Computers, a second hand shop selling all kinds of objects / collectables, and to this day operates as a micro-pub known as the 'Ilson Tap'.

The Ilson Tap micro pub at 162 Bath Street.

Guy Turner's furniture shop on the left and off the photo to the left was Healey's Chartered Surveyors.

West side of Bath Street between Manners Road & Pelham Street junctions. The shop nearest is James Coombes & Co., then A.H Whitmore & Sons followed by Foster Brothers Clothing Ltd at 63 Bath Street. Foster's had over 100 stores and claimed to be the cheapest in the world, selling blazer jackets, tennis shirts, jerseys, hats, caps, ties, underwear and their best selling collared Whitby and Albert Suits.

Photo taken from the junction of Bath Street with Pelham Street, circa. 1902. Note, the sign advertising 'Mrs Bull – A live paper for women which was available every Tuesday for 1d'.

Whiteheads & Co., Tailors & Outfitters at 134 Bath Street, Hodges & Co., Drapers at 136, the Bradford Warehouse Company Drapers at 138-140 and the Oyster Rooms.
Photo c.1902.

Dexter & Co., house furnishers at 133 Bath Street on the junction of Pelham Street & Bath Street. Members of the Dexter family can be seen standing to the front of the doorway. This photo was taken c.1904.

1968 – The Poplar Inn & Weaver to Wearer to the right, and near left Boots the chemist. Taylors, on the lower photograph moved into the Boots premises when Boots moved further up Bath Street having originally been located in the shop next door (off the photo).

Purpose built in the 1950's for Robinson's Fish & Poultry Shop, this shop has since been used as a Stationers and Tattoo Studio in the last decade or so. A common sight on the streets back then was the woman pushing the Manton (coach built) pram, the company Notman & Co., having been founded in Radford in the 1920's.
Photo taken c.1965.

1965 – The Poplar Inn & Trueform Shoes on the left, Burtons, Taylors & Boots the chemist on the right.

Looking north down Bath Street from the junction with Northgate Street c.1907.

The east side of Lower Bath Street from Northgate Street junction down to the entrance of Stamford Street. Includes Hedges Co. - Boots and Shoes, Home and Colonial Stores, Hudson's Provision Merchants, Singer Sewing Machine Co., J Rowell - Draper and the Cromwell Buildings. c.1901.

Melias Grocers Shop located at 112 Bath Street on the corner of Northgate Street.
Photo c.1925.

The Brunswick Hotel built in the 1860's, once stood at 74 Bath Street, the hotel closed in 1959 and was eventually replaced with the Midlands first Tesco 'Home N Wear' store in Sept 1961. Tesco remained in business until 1982 when the store finally closed. There has been several businesses on this site since, Specsavers being the latest.

A view of Bath Street in 1910 taken from the corner of Wilton Place. The United Counties Bank just off the photo to the left had been opened by one of its predecessors, the Nottingham & District Bank in 1891, then was rebuilt in 1896. The United Counties Bank took over in 1907, and was itself acquired by Barclays Bank in 1916.

The gentleman standing to the right of this photo is outside of the Brunswick Hotel, built in the 1860's. It was a very popular hotel with only the Rutland Arms being more popular at that time.

Middle Bath Street opposite Chapel Street - Fletcher Wine & Spirit Merchant, William Fletcher also operated as a chemist, druggist, ale merchant, mineral water manufacturer and bottler. William also owned the Erewash Valley Brewery which traded from nearby North Street. Photo c.1914.

A view down Bath Street from its junction with Station Road c.1910.

N.W Bradley the pork butchers operated until the 1980's before it became Rollinson's. Prior to Bradley operating from these premises, it was occupied by F.W Woolard in the early 1900's.
Central Radio Services and the New Inn P.H. can be seen to the right and Pounders on the opposite side of the road. Photo c.1949.

Tramcar No. 12 shown at the junction of Station Road and Bath Street, the fare costing 1/2d from Station Road to Bath Street and 1d elsewhere on the Cotmanhay to Hallam Fields route.

An era when most people never owned a television, but just rented them from shops such as Telefusion, Radio Rentals & Co-op Defiant. Fords can be seen opposite the junction of Station Road with Bath Street. Fords was great as a kid, a double fronted building with steps up from both sides of the shop to an upper floor, then another set of steps that wound around to a first floor that sold of vast array of kids toys. The smell of linen as you entered the shop is something that I'm sure most will fondly remember. Photo c.1963.

An old butchers shop on the corner of Chapel Street, the Prince of Wales public house to the right and six houses on Chapel Street were demolished in the early 1960's to make way for Burtons Supermarket, currently the site of Heron Foods.

Queues of people gathering on the far side of Bath Street awaiting the grand opening of Burtons Supermarket. Godber & Sons butchers and Smiths Dry Cleaners can be seen behind the crowds of people, and you also get a glimpse of a Daykin Row street sign on the south facing wall of Godber's butchers. Daykin Row once had a row of cottages running away to the west on the land currently occupied by St. Andrew's Church, this row of cottages derived its name from occupant John Daykin, a lace agent who died in the row in 1875.

Burtons Supermarket was constructed on the site of an old butches shop, the Prince of Wales P.H. and 6 houses on Chapel Street. This was the scene on its opening day back in the mid-60's. The building was later used by Fine Fare and Wilko's along with other stores.

Shoppers in Burtons Supermarket overwhelmed by the choice of foods on offer on the first day of opening. This view is shown taken from the back of the shop with the far window overlooking Bath Street. A special thanks goes out to Carl Aldred of Ilson Bygones for his kind permission to use his fathers photographs. Carl's father, Roy Aldred, worked for both Burtons and Fine Fare as a signwriter and was part of the team that produced the posters for the grand opening.

John Newton Saddle & Harness Maker, now the premises of House of Oliver Bridal Wear at 85 Bath Street.

Looking down Bath Street towards the junction with Chapel Street, Knowle Smith can be seen first, which was run by Joyce & Harry Briggs. This store was popular with women for their corsetry and underwear needs. Next was Wall Paper Stores Ltd, Curry's, Ferrand's, the Prince of Wales & an old butchers shop. Photo c.1957.

Smith Brothers Boot & Shoe occupied the Exchange Buildings at 66-68 Bath Street.
Photo c.1900.

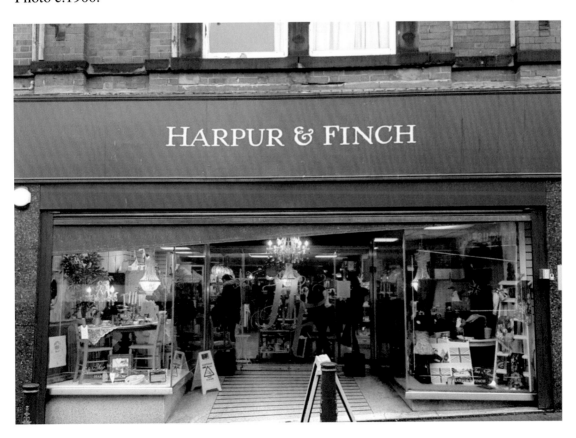

Looking down Bath Street towards the junction with Station Road. Marks & Spencer, Gunn's with the yellow advertising slogan above the window, Pounders – fashion shoes and Rose Shoe Shop on the junction. The five premises between Marks & Spencer and the corner of Station Road were all demolished to make way for Carlines store in the 60's. Carlines was one of Ilkeston's first supermarkets and was once managed by a Mr. Crisp. Diana Else of Ilkeston recalls that they bagged their own sugar in blue bags and patted their own butter in grease proof paper out of barrels.

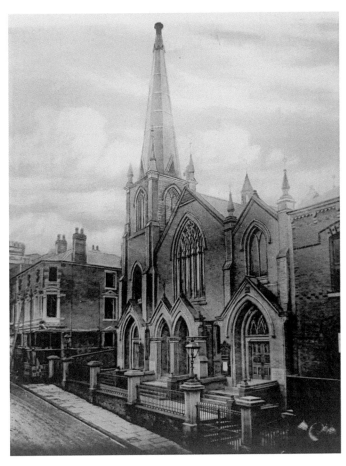

Bath Street Central Wesleyan Methodist Church.

The laying of the foundation stone took place on the 14th Oct 1896, the building was completed in 1898 and replaced an earlier building built in 1873 which stood behind this one.

In 1922 it became known as Central Mission or Central Methodist Church. The church finally closed its doors in May 1968 and was demolished in 1971.

A supermarket was built on this site and opened as Fine Fare in 1975, followed by Solo and then Wilkinson's since 1999.

This photo was taken circa. 1902, prior to this a cottage stood to the left of the Church.

1903 - Bath Street as viewed from the upper deck of a tram at the junction with Wilmot Street, Frederick Fletchers Wine and Spirit Merchant at 69 Bath Street can be seen to the left of the tram.

Bath Street in the very late 1800's / early 1900's, with Thomas Long 'Dyers & Dry Cleaners' at 35 Bath Street, William Small's butchers and Hooley's fried fish shop. All of these buildings have now long gone except for the buildings from the current Halifax Estates Agents down to the site of the old Army Stores which still remain.

The shop shown to the left was Jack Pillow's Wireless Store, the door to the right of this led to his daughter - Jeanne Pillow's School of Dance. Shortly afterwards this building was used by Browns Estate Agents and to this day is operated by the Halifax Estate Agents. The building shown to the right is the National Provincial Bank at 42 Bath Street.

1952 – Kings Picture House to the right was demolished in 1964, The King's was regarded as the most luxurious of Ilkeston's cinemas. Slightly further down Bath Street on the opposite side stood the short-lived Globe Cinema built in 1915 on the site of the former British School, which was latterly used as the Picture Palace. The Globe Cinema eventually closed its doors in 1923 after being purchased by F.W. Woolworth & Co.

National Provincial Bank to the right & Yeoman's Army Stores to the left.

The National Westminster Bank to the left of Albion Place started life as the Crompton and Evans Union Bank. Houses that originally stood on this site were demolished in 1892 to make way for the new bank. This joint stock banking company had been formed in June 1877 with the amalgamation of Messrs. Crompton, Newton & Co. of Derby and Chesterfield, and Messrs. W. and S. Evans & Co. of Derby.

Walter Lally, Boot Maker at 23 Bath Street and John Lally, Plumber on the opposite corner of Mount Street. Next door was Thomas Herbert Pickworth's musical instrument dealer and on the opposite side of Bath Street stood several cottages prior to the construction of Kings. Photo c.1914.

The Kings opened its doors to the public on March 22nd 1915, to become Ilkeston's second purpose-built cinema, beating the Globe by less than two months. Its name was derived after a visit by King George V to Ilkeston in 1914. The Kings soon established itself as the foremost picture house in the town and during its 49 year life was accepted by most as being the leading cinema in town.

The cinema was designed by local architect of Lord Haddon Road, H.Tatham Sudbury, the construction of the building was by Bosworth & Lowe of Nottingham.

The last showing at Kings was 'The Thrill of it All' starring Doris Day.

Kings Picture House – photo taken just after closure in March 1964.

View down Bath Street from just above the entry to the yard of Carrier's Factory (to the right). Shops; H Higgitt, Outfitter; T.H Pickworth Musical Instruments; and George Adams, Florist. The twin gables and steps of the British School can be seen to the rear of the horse and cart. c.1901.

Star Tea Co., Ltd at 19 Bath Street & H Higgitt, Outfitter. c.1901.

Thomas Hickinbotham milliners – top west side at 17 Bath Street, In later years Hickinbotham set up business on the junction of Heanor Road and Granby Street within the same building as the Pearl Assurance Company. Photo c.1901.

The Girl Guides Patrol can be seen entering Bath Street by the side of the Harrow Inn – c.1912.

East Street & Burr Lane

Photo believed to have been taken during the Celebration of Queen Victoria's Diamond Jubilee 1897.

The three storey buildings seen to both sides of the street have long since disappeared, those to the right having been demolished to make way for the construction of the Derby Savings Bank in 1937/38. The main doorway which can be seen to the front of the Wine Vaults was later bricked up due to a number of incidents involving the steep steps that once led up to the pub. A door to the west side of the building then became the main entrance.

The Gladstone Inn - A licenced premises for the sale of beer since the early 1830's.

In the early 1860's this plot was listed as having a brew house, piggery, stables, kitchen building & slaughter house as well as three adjoining cottages – Photo taken 1964.

In later years this building at East Street operated as Ilkeston Sauna run by a lady known as 'Scotch Jenny'. The building has fallen into a poor state over the years and has recently been offered for sale.

Burr Lane looking north, all of the houses on the east side were demolished to make way for the construction of Chalons Way in 1992/93.

Burr Lane as viewed from Byron Street in 1984

The same view taken from Byron Street but with the houses on Burr Lane obscured by the wall on Chalons Way (inner relief road). Chalons Way was constructed in 1992/93 and literally cut Ilkeston in half. The works resulted in the loss of many streets and houses around the area to the rear of Market Street all the way down to the end of Stamford Street / North Street. At the top end of Chalons Way, unfortunately many of our dead had to be reinterred due to the loss of St. Mary's Churchyard extension being bulldozed in the process.

Chapel Street, North Street, Station Road & Station Street

The Flowerpot public house on Chapel Street, demolished in the early 90's around the same time as the construction of Chalons Way (inner relief road). This was a very popular Shipstones pub in its day, but like many streets and properties that disappeared during the early 90's this was one of those unfortunately targeted.

The Erewash Hotel at 23 Station Road and the surrounding streets looked quite different before the construction of Chalons Way. With North Street running down to the east side of the pub and Chapel Street, in the forefront, running west towards Bath Street. North Street has now all but disappeared apart from the short span that can still be seen between the pub and Chalons Way.

A view looking north across Chapel Street with the buildings on Station Road in the distance. Today there is Albion Street that leads up from Station Road cutting through Chapel Street providing access to parking at the bottom end of the Albion Shopping Centre.

This block of shops on Station Road was built in 1899, and can be found to the west of the Erewash Hotel. At No.17 was Whiteheads – Fruit & Veg shop, next door was Goya Hair Styles & C.Cable Newsagents. In the late 80's, Quick Kitchen Fish & Chip Restaurant set up business at No.17 and in the early 90's Stephen Brown opened Alpha – Disco & Music Instruments which is still operating to this day. Stephen has lived above the shop since April 1964. Photo taken 1985.

The Erewash Hotel at the junction with Station Road & North Street.

Chalons Way relief road under construction 1992/93.

Now known as the Dew Drop Inn, the Middleton Hotel at Ilkeston Junction was named after the landowner Baron Middleton of Warwickshire – built in 1884.

Rumour has it that the upper floor was removed due to a fire that caused extensive damage.

Upper & Lower Market places

Celebration of Queen Victoria's Diamond Jubilee 1897 – Town Hall and cottages prior to the construction of Wharncliffe Road.

In May 1866 the Local Board bought a row of thatched cottages from John Taylor of Ilkeston Manor House for £800 for the purpose of building a town hall.

The Town Hall was built between 1866 and 1868 by Mr Warner of Ilkeston who also built the Unitarian Chapel (now the Masonic Hall) at about the same time. The design was by Charles Sutton, a renowned Nottingham architect. Sutton later designed Francis Sudbury & Sons hosiery factory on Market Street in 1881. Photo 1890.

The Lord of the Manor, the Duke of Rutland, laid the foundation stone on the 27th September 1866 and the opening ceremony took place on 6th February 1868.

Joseph Wrights Barbers stood at No.1 the Market Place until 1937 when it was demolished to make way for the expansion of the Ilkeston Co-operative Society up to the corner of Wharncliffe Road.

During this demolition the block containing the old Post Office, the Barbers & the Bon-bon shop once owned by William Topley Richards all disappeared.

As can be seen in this photo, the Town Hall has been through many changes, extending to the south & west sides.

Ilkeston's War Memorial – Designed and created by Mr H Tatham Sudbury & Messrs Pask and Thorpe. Unveiled on the 8th Jan 1922 with the names of 467 casualties of the First World War, Unveiled a second time on the 10th Sept 1950 with an additional 175 names of those lost in the Second World War. Site restored with new railings and raised flower beds 1994/95. Top photo c.1926.

Ilkeston's St. Mary's church dates from the early 13th century. The original spire on the tower was destroyed by a lightning strike in 1714.

The church was extensively restored between 1853 and 1855 by Thomas Larkins Walker. The north and south aisles were rebuilt, and they were restored to their original length towards the west. The chantry chapel was rebuilt to accommodate a further 300 people. The chancel arch was restored and the tower was re-cased. A new vestry was added on the foundations of the old sacristry, adjoining the south wall of the chapel. New seating and flooring was fitted, and new heating and lighting was installed. The contractor was Lindley and Fearn of Leicester. It was reopened on 18 October 1855.

The west end was enlarged and rebuilt between 1909 and 1910 by Percy Heylyn Currey. It reopened for worship on 20 September 1910 by the Bishop of Southwell.

Top photo c.1902 – Note the church prior to the enlargement which can be clearly seen by the length of the roof to the rear of the tower.

Lifeboat Saturday Celebrations – 1909.

The procession started at Skeavington's Lane in Cotmanhay, it can be seen heading in the direction of Wharncliffe Road towards the Pimlico Recreation, known to us today as Rutland Recreational Ground (Rutland Rec).

Late 1950's – Other than becoming pedestrianised in 1993, the Market Place has remained pretty much unchanged except for the usage of some of the buildings, and alterations to the ground floor frontage of the Town Hall.

The Ilkeston "Carnegie Free Library", built over 100 years ago, the library looks almost the same today except for the missing pediments that became unsafe, hence their removal in later years. In 1904, readers selected their books from lists and it was not until 1922 that they were allowed to browse the shelves themselves.

Awarded Grade II listing in 1986.

A typical Ilkeston Market day in 1903.

Photo late 1878, Kings Head, Sutton and Co. and Market Tavern.

Jedediah Wigley, known as Jerry Wigley built two shops, the first being what is now Eclipse Hair Salon and the building on the opposite side of the alleyway. Within the building to the left, his daughter Sophia Wigley had a millinery and dressmaking business to the front, whilst the Market Inn Tavern stood to the rear accessed via a door facing into the alleyway.

In 1878 what is now the left hand side of the Market Inn and Shakers Cocktail Bar were part of the same building. Only in the last decade has the left hand side of the Market Inn been re-opened up to transform this building back to how it was originally built.

Lower Market Place circa. 1906 with the Liberal Club and Dr. Wood's Surgery in the background, now the site of the Lloyds Bank and the Observatory P.H. Just off the photo to the right were the underground lavatories that opened in 1899 and closed in the mid-1920's.

On the far left of this photo is the Market Inn and Eclipse Hairdressers which for many decades was Bartons Fruit & Veg Shop known to many Ilkestonian's.

Crawford's Commercial Café – Sometime during the late 1930's it became Richards Hairdressing Salon, Walter occupied the ground floor for the gents, whilst Doris (known to most people as 'Dolly') had the first floor, the top floor having been used for bedrooms until the mid to late 1950's.

My father said he was always amused when Walt would ask "Anything for the weekend sir", when paying for his haircut – I can't imagine what he meant!

They later set up home on Kniveton Park and shortly afterwards, the upper floor was converted to a salon so that Doris had salons on both upper floors. Prior to running this salon in the early 1930's, Walter, or 'Walt' as he was better known, had a hairdressers and tobacconists on Alvenor Street.

After the closure of the hairdressing salon, Fred Davey, formerly of the Market Inn opened Davey's Bookmakers, Safeway Electrical then operated from the premises from 1982 until it finally became Shakers Cocktail Bar in 2005.

Greenhough & Johnson Ironmongers at 16 Bath Street was owned by the well known William Merry who was a chemist and ironmonger while Messrs Greenhough and Johnson were his assistants. The business began trading in 1894 and continued well into the late 1950's even after the death of Mr Greenhough in 1944.

1960 – Demolition of Ilkeston's Liberal Club, formerly the site of the old Anchor Inn which served only for a short while from 1789.

The Liberal Club in the Lower Market Place is yet another landmark lost to the town.

Its heyday was the period from about 1906 to 1918, when the club had about 500 members and was the headquarters of Sir Walter Foster, Liberal M.P.

Replaced with the P&D Store, then the supermarket Kwik Save which was eventually converted to create the Observatory pub as we know it today.

1920 – View looking west towards the upper market place.

The Harrow Inn to the left at the top of Bath Street, Dr Robert Wood M.R.C.S Eng L.S.A. Consulting Surgeon & Certifying Factory Surgeon at 10 Market Place – the steps to the right of the photo leading to his front door. The building on the south corner of East Street and the lower market place was E.Sutton Estate Agents / Accountants with a butchers shop underneath. Behind this on the opposite corner of East Street the Borough Arms P.H can just be seen. Photo 1905.

The Old Harrow Inn stood on the west-side of Bath Street at the opening onto the lower market place. It was bought by Ilkeston Borough Council then later demolished and rebuilt in 1896 as part of an improvement plan, as it would cause problems with the trams negotiating the tight bend onto Bath Street. The distance between the Harrow Inn and Dr Wood's Surgery also made the lower market place less attractive when viewed from Bath Street. George Webster & Samuel Gothard's Chemist can be seen to the left at 16 Market Place. Photo c.1887.

1911 – Coronation of King George V.
Dr. Wood can be seen on horseback heading down towards Bath Street.

The old underground toilets uncovered in 1993 as shown in this photograph, taken during the revamp of Ilkeston Market Place. These toilets had been in operation from circa. 1899 until the mid-1920's.

There were two sets of steps leading down against the church wall, the wall had white tiles attached to it which can be clearly seen on the photo. Natural daylight was provided to these subterranean toilets via glass panels on the ground. Unfortunately these toilets were quickly filled in again as not to draw too much attention to the general public.

Pimlico

The Scala Picture House on Pimlico soon after opening in 1913. A group of local business men, Messrs Starr, Severn (Arthur Severn on photo), Wilcock, Colclough, and Brookes decided that the town could support a second picture house. They purchased the Burns Street Independent Chapel graveyard on the corner of Burns Street and Pimlico and built what was to become Ilkeston's first purpose-built cinema.

Pimlico looking east with the Sir John Warren on the right, the Kings Head in the centre and Dorothy Cottages to the left. Photo believed to be mid-1950's.

The open-air baths on Wharncliffe Road, which served the town from August 1921 until the completion of the Manners Road swimming pools in 1972.

These open-air baths stood on the site of the old Victorian fire station which was to the rear (west-side) of the Town Hall.

Market Street

Market Street in 1901, the dentists and Rutland Garments to the left and café to right.

Alan Clifton's old second-hand shop on the east side of Market Street in the 1980's, I spent a fair amount of my pocket money on singles & LP's's in here over the years. Now converted to a residency.

Market Street at the junction with Gladstone Street (West & East), properties to the left include Dennis Tapp & Co., Seed Merchants in what is now the Burnt Pig Ale Ouse, Owen Bostock – Tobacconist just above at 51 Market Street. & H. Thorpe & Sons at 54. Photo c.1910.

This photograph was taken at the south end of Market Street. This site had been cleared for a proposed bus station to be built on the site of the former health centre.

The house opposite at No.15 Market Street was demolished in the early 90's to make way for Chalons Way – Ilkeston's Relief Road.

Just to the left of where No. 15 stood (opposite the current Burnt Pig Ale Ouse) was the old Wesleyan Chapel, founded in 1880 and closed in 1889. The windows from this chapel were removed and used in a new-build chapel on Stamford Street. Shortly afterwards the chapel on Market Street was demolished.

Photo taken - 1979

South Street

Sydney Thorpe House Furnisher at 16 South Street, he also had showrooms on Coronation Street & Market Street. The Post Office can be seen on the left which was built in 1917 and replaced the old Post Office which once stood on the Market Place next to J.Wrights Barbers. The Ritz Cinema can be seen on the opposite side of the junction with Coronation Street.

J.F. Walker – Printers, bookseller & fancy goods dealer to the left, then Sydney Thorpe's and the old Sunday Schoolrooms next door which was later purchased by the Ilkeston Co-operative Society. The Post Office and the Library can be seen on the right.

Photo early 1936 - Cottage prior to demolition, replaced with the Ritz Cinema in 1937/38.

South Street c.1910 at the junction with Queen Street. The garden wall on the left surrounds what is now the USA Kentucky Chicken premises. On the right, can be seen the vacant land on which the present day Hogarth's Public House stands.

Built as the General Baptist Chapel in 1853, now known as Queen Street Baptist Church.
Photo above c.1901.

1983 – The Nags Head just prior to becoming Thorpes.
Some of the previous landlords/ladies over the years include Sarah Clay, Albert Roberts, Colin and Marlene Harrison and Fred Davey to name just a few.

Photo believed to be c.1913.

The Nags Head can be seen on the immediate left, after this were three cottages at 32-36 South Street and further up the road after Queens Street stood J.E.Callinan - Hairdressers, William Gough - Fruiterers & Greengrocers, Mrs V.S. Barker – Confectioners, Sydney Thorpe and the School Rooms (owned by the Ilkeston Co-operative Society).

Within the three-storey building to the right, at 43-45 (now Truly Scrumptious, the Worx & Tudor Jewellers) was Arthur Beardsley – Taylors and Clothiers & next door at 45 was A.Mosely – Dyers & Cleaners.

A view looking up South Street from close to the junction with West Street. The shops to the left were J.H.Sentence – Drapers at 52-52A and J.Broadhurst – Grocers a little further up before the Nags Head pub. On the right side at the junction with Gladstone Street (west) was Jolly & Waltham – Confectioners. Photo taken during the winter of 1930.

South Street in 1909. Ben Cope's Carrier horse and cart can be seen outside of Merry's Chemist. Ben Cope is still operating to this day from the same business premises as he was over 100 years ago at 28 Belper Street. On the opposite side of the road is the Prince of Wales P.H. which was ran by Eli Barrett.

The Trueman's business started up c.1929 on Granby Street in Ilkeston then moved to South Street in the mid-1960's. The business was run by Frank Trueman until his passing in the mid-60's, then his son John took over the shop. Alan Hobson worked in the shop for 35 years from leaving school until around the year 2000, he then left to start his own decorating business for the next 7 years. Since 2008, Alan has moved to warmer climates living in Trinidad.

The last of Ilkeston's thatched cottages owned by the Sanders family on the corner of Derby Road and South Street. This property remained in the family for over 130 years. Mr Sanders worked from this address as a Market Gardener; a lot of the produce sold coming from 'Sanders Orchard' which stood on the site now occupied by St. Andrews Drive. Mr Sanders also had an additional shop opposite Brussels Terrace on Bath Street.

The cottage was purchased by Premier Garage Co., Ilkeston and demolished in 1934. (c.1907).

White Lion Square

The White Lion Square as viewed from the corner of Derby Road and South Street. In the distance to the left can be seen the White Lion and Travellers Rest pubs. To the right of the Travellers rest stood a Chemists. To the right of the photo are the officers of the Derbyshire and Nottinghamshire Electric Power Company - this building having been designed by Ilkeston Architect Harry Tatham Sudbury. See also the overhead wires of the trolley buses (known to most as trackless), in service from 1932-53.
Photo taken 1939.

The White Lion Square in the early 1990's prior to the construction of Chalons Way, the White Lion having already been demolished. The other building to the right being the Travellers Rest, J. Bramley's Hardware Store which had operated for over 80 years, and Thorpes which can now be found in the building of the Old Nags Head Pub on South Street.

John Smiths Butchers in c.1984, stood on the corner of Nottingham Road opposite the White Lion pub which if still here to this day would have been one of Ilkeston's oldest pubs, if not the oldest (formerly known as the Fighting Cocks).

Prior to the butchers being run by John Smith, it had been Greenaway's in the early 60's, where people would form a queue outside waiting for his speciality savoury duck, shortly afterwards it became Spendloves & then Attenborough's.

Apollo 'the bargain makers' at the junction of Park Road and White Lion Square was a bargain store for clothes and other goods. The building was constructed in 1923 as Premier Garage for car sales on the lower floor with a ball room on the upper floor. In later years it was known as the Premier Dance Hall and then the Catholic Club. Many people have reminisced of rock & roll bands that played there three nights a week. Johnny Clay's band on Saturday nights and Eric Raymonde and his Orchestra. When people weren't partying the night away here they'd be at Graingers on Corporation Road as they also had regular rock & roll nights.

In the late 70's / 80's it became very popular for its Judo classes.

Stanton Road & Little Hallam Hill

Stanton Road Cemetery with house and chapel of rest. The cemetery opened in 1866 and became the resting place of well known Ilkestonian Samuel Taylor - Ilkeston's Giant who stood at an astonishing 7ft 4-1/2" tall, Samuel was born in Little Hallam in 1816.– Photo taken in 1962.

The Bulls Head Inn, Little Hallam Hill which was formerly called the Anchor. The Inn was rechristened as the Bulls Head Inn after it was re-mortgaged on the 24th April, 1810 for the sum of £450. This was one of three Anchor Pubs that once stood in Ilkeston since the late 1780's, the others being on the lower Market Place & Market Street.

View looking east up Little Hallam Hill, the 'Brooklands' can be seen nearest right and Little Hallam Farm to the rear. The bridge crossing the road carried the mineral railway line from the Derby to Nottingham branch of the Great Northern Railway line to Stanton Ironworks. Photo 1914.